INSIDE THE NFL

# MIAMI DOLPHINS

by Charlie Beattie

Abdo & Daughters
MIDDLE GRADE NONFICTION
An imprint of Abdo Publishing
abdobooks.com

ABDOBOOKS.COM

Published by Abdo Publishing, a division of ABDO, PO Box 398166, Minneapolis, Minnesota 55439.


Printed in China.
052025
092025

THIS BOOK CONTAINS RECYCLED MATERIALS

Cover Photos: Thearon W. Henderson/Getty Images Sport/Getty Images (Tua Tagovailoa); George Gojkovich/Getty Images Sport/Getty Images (Dan Marino)
Interior Photos: Michael Owens/Getty Images Sport/Getty Images, 4–5; Mark Brown/Getty Images Sport/Getty Images, 6; David Ramos/Getty Images Sport/Getty Images, 7; Rich Storry/Getty Images Sport/Getty Images, 8; Harry How/Getty Images Sport/Getty Images, 9, 61 (bottom right); Abdo Publishing, 10–11, 58; Focus on Sport/Getty Images, 12–13, 19, 22–23, 26, 29, 32, 63; Lynne Sladky/AP Images, 14; AP Images, 15, 35, 60 (top); Al Messerschmidt Archive/AP Images, 16, 38–39, 42, 60 (bottom right); Focus on Sport/Getty Images Sport/Getty Images, 18, 27, 31, 34, 40, 60 (bottom left); James Flores/Getty Images Sport/Getty Images, 20; Tony Tomsic/AP Images, 21, 25; Ross Lewis/Getty Images Sport/Getty Images, 24; Nate Fine/Getty Images Sport/Getty Images, 28; Jacquelyn Martin/AP Images, 30; Bettmann/Getty Images, 33; Michael Zagaris/Getty Images Sport/Getty Images, 36–37; Paul Spinelli/AP Images, 41; George Gojkovich/Getty Images Sport/Getty Images, 43; George Rose/Getty Images Sport/Getty Images, 44, 46, 61 (bottom left); Doug Jennings/AP Images, 45; Paul Spinelli/NFL Photos/AP Images, 47; Tom DiPace/AP Images, 48–49, 61 (top left); Gregory Shamus/Getty Images Sport/Getty Images, 51; Eliot J. Schechter/Getty Images Sport/Getty Images, 52; Wilfredo Lee/AP Images, 53, 54; Rick Stewart/Getty Images Sport/Getty Images, 55; Jim Davis/Boston Globe/Getty Images, 56, 61 (top right); Peter Joneleit/Icon Sportswire/Getty Images, 57; Megan Briggs/Getty Images Sport/Getty Images, 59

Editor: Chrös McDougall
Series Designer: Laura Graphenteen
Production Designer: Katharine Hale

**Library of Congress Control Number: 2024948465**

**Publisher's Cataloging-in-Publication Data**

Names: Beattie, Charlie, author.
Title: Miami Dolphins / by Charlie Beattie
Description: Minneapolis, Minnesota: Abdo Publishing, 2026 | Series: Inside the NFL | Includes online resources and index.
Identifiers: ISBN 9781098296810 (lib. bdg.) | ISBN 9798384919339 (ebook)
Subjects: LCSH: Miami Dolphins (Football team)--Juvenile literature. | National Football League--Juvenile literature. | Football teams--Juvenile literature. | American football--Juvenile literature.
Classification: DDC 796.33264--dc23

# CONTENTS

The Miami Dolphins' Tyreek Hill is one of the most dangerous receivers in the NFL.

CHAPTER 1

# THE CHEETAH

**TYREEK HILL LIKES TO DO THINGS IN A HURRY. THE MIAMI DOLPHINS** receiver is one of the fastest players in the National Football League (NFL). And in Week 1 of the 2023 season, he was ready to get off to a flying start.

The Dolphins were in Los Angeles taking on the Chargers. After a back-and-forth first half, Los Angeles scored a touchdown to go up 24–20 midway through the third quarter. That score remained as Hill lined up on the right side of the formation with 2:18 left in the quarter. Surveying the defense, Hill knew he had one-on-one coverage from Los Angeles cornerback J. C. Jackson. The Miami speedster, whose nickname is "Cheetah," dug his cleats into the turf and waited for the snap. Fans looked on, waiting to see what the speed demon would do next.

**Hill arrived in Miami in 2022 as a three-time All-Pro and Super Bowl champion.**

## AIMING HIGH

Hill had first made a name for himself with the Kansas City Chiefs. Though only a fifth-round draft pick in 2016, he quickly established himself as an elite downfield threat. Over six seasons in Kansas City, he made six Pro Bowls and helped the Chiefs win a Super Bowl. Then, prior to the 2022 season, the Dolphins traded for him.

Hill wasted no time introducing himself to the long-suffering fans of south Florida. The team had reached the playoffs only twice in the previous 20 seasons. With Hill catching deep shots from young quarterback Tua Tagovailoa, the Dolphins ended that streak in 2022. Along the way, Hill rewrote Miami's record book. He caught a team-record 119 passes, and his 1,710 receiving yards smashed the old mark by more than 300.

Hill entered the 2023 season with lofty goals. He said he'd like to become the first NFL receiver to ever top 2,000 yards in a season. To get there, Hill needed to get off to a fast start in Week 1.

## THE BLUR

As he lined up across from Jackson, Hill knew where he was headed next: the end zone. Tagovailoa took the snap at the Los Angeles 35-yard line. With Jackson starting just a few yards away, Hill made a quick juke, shaking his shoulders to the inside of the field. The defender bit on the fake, and Hill broke to the outside and took off.

Tagovailoa instantly saw Hill get open on the outside. The left-handed quarterback lofted a ball over the head of both players. He knew that Hill, who was once clocked at a running speed of 23.3 miles per hour (37.4 km/h), had the wheels to get there. Sure enough, the 5-foot-10, 191-pound Hill sprinted under the ball, cradling it in his arms just as he crossed the goal line for the go-ahead touchdown.

The catch was just one part of a huge day for Hill. He ended the game with

### TRACK STAR

Tyreek Hill was a track star before he joined the NFL. In high school, he won the Georgia state championships in both the 100 and 200 meters and nearly set a national high school record in the 200. He then went to Garden City Community College in Kansas. In a national meet in 2013, Hill broke the 10-second mark in the 100 meters, finishing with a time of 9.98 seconds.

Hill, *left*, celebrates his second-place finish in the 200 meters at a meet in Barcelona, Spain, in 2012.

Hill makes one of his NFL-leading 13 touchdown catches in 2023.

11 catches and 215 yards. That was the fourth-highest receiving total for a season opener in NFL history. And among those catches was another touchdown—this one the game winner. Hill's 4-yard reception with 1:45 left gave the Dolphins a 36–34 victory.

"I wanted to play fast and deliberate," Hill said. "I kind of went into a zone there."

> **"I WANTED TO PLAY FAST AND DELIBERATE. I KIND OF WENT INTO A ZONE THERE."**
>
> —TYREEK HILL

Though Hill ultimately came up short of his 2,000-yard goal, he still broke his own Dolphins single-season record with 1,799 receiving yards. And he did so despite missing a game. Had he been able to compete in all 17 games, the Cheetah may have sprinted his way to NFL history.

Hill hauls in the game-winning touchdown in the final minutes against the Los Angeles Chargers.

# NFL TEAMS MAP

## NFC

### NFC EAST

- DALLAS COWBOYS
- NEW YORK GIANTS
- PHILADELPHIA EAGLES
- WASHINGTON COMMANDERS

### NFC WEST

- ARIZONA CARDINALS
- LOS ANGELES RAMS
- SAN FRANCISCO 49ERS
- SEATTLE SEAHAWKS

### NFC NORTH

- CHICAGO BEARS
- DETROIT LIONS
- GREEN BAY PACKERS
- MINNESOTA VIKINGS

### NFC SOUTH

- ATLANTA FALCONS
- CAROLINA PANTHERS
- NEW ORLEANS SAINTS
- TAMPA BAY BUCCANEERS

# AFC

## AFC EAST

- BUFFALO BILLS
- MIAMI DOLPHINS
- NEW ENGLAND PATRIOTS
- NEW YORK JETS

## AFC WEST

- DENVER BRONCOS
- KANSAS CITY CHIEFS
- LAS VEGAS RAIDERS
- LOS ANGELES CHARGERS

## AFC NORTH

- BALTIMORE RAVENS
- CINCINNATI BENGALS
- CLEVELAND BROWNS
- PITTSBURGH STEELERS

## AFC SOUTH

- HOUSTON TEXANS
- INDIANAPOLIS COLTS
- JACKSONVILLE JAGUARS
- TENNESSEE TITANS

Joe Robbie owned the Dolphins from 1966 until his death in 1990.

CHAPTER 2

# FOOTBALL BY THE BEACH

**The NFL was founded in 1920, and by the late 1950s, it had** become a popular and successful league. One thing the NFL owners didn't want, however, was more teams. So in 1960, a group of prospective new owners created the American Football League (AFL) to challenge the NFL. Though the new league considered putting a team in Miami, it elected to go to Buffalo in upstate New York instead. The dream of pro football in the sunny south-Florida city never died, though.

To the surprise of many, the AFL proved it could compete with the NFL for players and fans. By 1966, the NFL worked out a deal with the AFL to merge. The two league champions would meet at the end of the season in what's now known as Super Bowl I, and the two leagues would officially become one in 1970. To make everything work, though, the AFL needed more teams. It had only eight franchises, compared with the 14 in the NFL.

Miami was determined not to miss its second chance. Lawyer Joe Robbie led the charge for the expansion team. Originally from South Dakota, Robbie was a passionate football fan willing to do what it took to secure a franchise. But he didn't have enough money on his own. To fix that problem, he teamed up with actor and comedian Danny Thomas. The famous Miami native helped get Robbie's dream off the ground, and the AFL kicked off in Miami in 1966.

## STEPPING ON SHELLS

Even with Thomas's financial backing, the newly formed Dolphins weren't swimming in money. The team was so financially limited that

**The Dolphins played their home games at the Miami Orange Bowl from 1966 to 1986.**

Running back Joe Auer, *center*, scored nine touchdowns for the Dolphins in 1966.

it practiced at a local high school. As the school was near the ocean, players complained of stepping on shells that had drifted in off the nearby beach.

Robbie and Thomas tabbed veteran coach George Wilson as Miami's first head coach. He inherited a team full of colorful personalities. Linebacker Wahoo McDaniel was a successful professional wrestler who once took off from training camp for a championship bout in the ring. McDaniel was also the only player in professional football who wore his nickname on the back of his jersey. Meanwhile, running back Joe Auer owned a pet lion.

Auer provided the team's first on-field thrill. On September 2, 1966, he returned the first kickoff in Miami history 95 yards for a touchdown. But excitement proved hard to come by in those first seasons. Sporting one of the league's worst defenses, the Dolphins had a combined record of 15–39–2 in their first four seasons.

## THE NEW BOSS

By the end of the 1960s, Miami needed a new coach. In 1969, the team caught a lucky break. Don Shula had been a successful coach with the NFL's Baltimore Colts. In January of that year, his team reached Super Bowl III, where the Colts were huge favorites over the AFL's New York Jets. When Baltimore lost the game in a shocking upset, Shula's relationship with team owner Carroll Rosenbloom soured. Sensing an opportunity, Robbie and the Dolphins lured the 40-year-old coach to Miami in time for the 1970 season.

Right away, Shula's players noticed a difference in styles from the Wilson era. Wilson ran loose practices, or sometimes none at all. Shula ran a tight ship and worked his players hard at training camp, even in Florida's withering summer heat. "With George Wilson, if it was too hot, we went swimming," said running back Mercury Morris.

**The Dolphins gave up their top draft pick in 1970 to sign Don Shula as head coach.**

"With Don Shula, we didn't have a drink of water on the field in seven years."

> **"WITH DON SHULA, WE DIDN'T HAVE A DRINK OF WATER ON THE FIELD IN SEVEN YEARS."**
>
> **—MERCURY MORRIS**

Shula's methods might have been harsh, but he turned Miami into a winning team. In 1970, the Dolphins finished 10–4 and reached the playoffs for the first time. Although they fell to the Oakland Raiders 21–14 in the divisional round, the future finally looked bright in Miami.

## THE LONGEST GAME

Shula wasn't the only reason for Miami's new success. Player personnel director Joe Thomas had been with the team since the beginning. During the team's early struggles, he was putting together the core of a future champion.

Miami drafted running backs Larry Csonka and Jim Kiick in 1968 and Morris a year later. The speedy Morris, powerful Csonka, and versatile Kiick soon made up one of the NFL's best backfields. Handing them the ball was steady quarterback Bob Griese, the team's top pick in 1967. The offensive line featured three standouts in center Jim Langer and guards Bob Kuechenberg and Larry Little. Morris liked to say the trio didn't open up holes, but rather they opened hallways for runners to go through.

### FLIPPER

In Miami's first three seasons, a live dolphin mascot named Flipper entertained fans from her tank behind one of the end zones. Flipper would retrieve kicks that landed in her tank. She would also do flips whenever the Dolphins scored. However, because the team's offense struggled so much, Flipper began to perform after every successful first down. Flipper retired back to the Miami Aquarium in 1968 when it became too expensive to maintain her tank at the field.

Thomas also brought in receiving threat Paul Warfield, a former Cleveland Browns star, in a 1970 trade.

All-Pro linebacker Nick Buoniconti arrived in 1969 to anchor the defense. He joined defensive linemen Vern Den Herder and Bill Stanfill and safeties Dick Anderson and Jake Scott to form the core of an improving unit. In 1971, the Dolphins allowed the third-fewest points in the NFL as they finished 10–3–1 to win their first division title.

In the playoff opener, Miami traveled to Kansas City to face the Chiefs on Christmas. Behind rushing touchdowns from both Csonka and Kiick, the Dolphins battled back from an early 10–0 hole to tie the game 17–17 heading into the fourth quarter. After Kansas City pulled ahead again, Griese tossed a 5-yard touchdown pass late in the fourth to tie the game 24–24.

The teams went into overtime, and the game dragged on as both sides missed potential

Linebacker Nick Buoniconti was the first Dolphins defensive player to make the Hall of Fame.

Offensive lineman Larry Little was named to the All-Pro team each season from 1971 to 1975.

game-winning field goal attempts. When one overtime wasn't enough, some players were worried the game wouldn't end. "I lost so much weight that day that my pants were loose," said Csonka, who estimated that he dropped 18 pounds (8 kg).

After 82 minutes of game action, it was by far the longest game in professional football history. The Dolphins had the ball and went to a play they used frequently. It was called "Roll Right, Trap Left." Miami hadn't run the play all game because the coaches were sure the Chiefs were looking for it. The play was designed to fool the defense into thinking the run would go to the right. Then the Dolphins would reverse direction once the defense committed. It worked perfectly as Csonka burst through a big hole for 29 yards. A few plays later, Miami kicker Garo Yepremian ended the marathon by hitting a 37-yard field goal to secure a 27–24 win.

Miami wide receiver Paul Warfield led the NFL with 11 touchdown receptions in 1971.

## SUPER DISAPPOINTMENT

A week later, the Dolphins faced Shula's old Colts team for the American Football Conference (AFC) title. Baltimore arrived as the defending Super Bowl champion. The Dolphins were ready. Griese and Warfield got things started with a 75-yard touchdown connection in the first quarter. From there, Miami's defense took over. In the third quarter, Anderson intercepted a pass at the Miami 25. Not known for his speed, Anderson nonetheless took off down the right sideline, following punishing blocks by his teammates for a touchdown.

After the game, Buoniconti joked that he had time to get a hot dog from the concession stand in the time it took Anderson to reach the end zone. Anderson joked back, "That's because you were the only one who didn't make a block." Csonka ran for another touchdown in the fourth quarter to seal a 21–0 victory and give Shula another shot at the big game.

However, the Dolphins flopped in Super Bowl VI. Facing a sturdy Dallas Cowboys defense, Miami's offense never got going. On one play in the second quarter that summed up Miami's day, Griese tried to scramble away from two defenders. He retreated so much that by the time the Cowboys sacked him he had lost 29 yards.

**Defensive back Dick Anderson had 34 interceptions and 16 fumble recoveries during his career with the Dolphins.**

The Dolphins lost 24–3, becoming the first team not to reach the end zone in the Super Bowl. It took nearly 50 years for another team to do that. Bitter about the defeat, the embarrassed Dolphins returned in 1972 with a vow to take it all the way.

Dolphins linebacker Nick Buoniconti, *center*, fires up members of "the No-Name Defense."

CHAPTER 3

# PERFECTION

**In the buildup to Super Bowl VI, reporters had asked** Dallas Cowboys coach Tom Landry about Miami's defense. He responded by saying that the Dolphins had good defensive players, but he couldn't name them. With that, "the No-Name Defense" was born.

Despite the name, the Dolphins boasted some elite defensive talent. In 1972, All-Pro defensive end Bill Stanfill joined Vern Den Herder and Manny Fernandez to provide a fierce pass rush. Linebacker Nick Buoniconti covered the ground behind them. He finished as the runner-up for the league's Defensive Player of the Year Award. Meanwhile, safeties Dick Anderson and Jake Scott totaled eight of the team's 26 interceptions.

Defensive coordinator Bill Arnsparger guided the unit. He often used creative wrinkles to catch

Dolphins running back Mercury Morris charges upfield during a 1972 game.

opponents off guard. One of them, called the "53" defense, was named after linebacker Bob Matheson's jersey number. Matheson didn't play every down, but when he came on, the 28-year-old would line up all over the Dolphins' formation. From there, he created tough matchups for opposing offensive lines who suddenly didn't have enough blockers for a certain spot.

## CHASING PERFECTION

The Dolphins started the 1972 season 5–0, but quarterback Bob Griese suffered an ankle injury in the fifth win. Few thought the team's perfect start would last with 38-year-old backup Earl Morrall taking over under center. In Griese's absence, the Dolphins leaned on their three-headed rushing attack of Larry Csonka, Jim Kiick, and Mercury Morris. Csonka and Morris both topped 1,000 yards as Miami led the league in both rushing yards and touchdowns. Meanwhile, the No-Name Defense held opponents to the NFL's lowest scoring average.

The Dolphins admitted that their strategy of steady running plays and solid defense wasn't all that exciting to watch. But heading into the final day of the season, the Dolphins were 13–0. They welcomed coach Don Shula's old Baltimore Colts to Miami's Orange Bowl and put on a superb performance. In the second quarter, Morrall connected on a 14-yard touchdown pass to receiver Paul Warfield for the game's only touchdown. Kicker Garo Yepremian added three field goals. And the No-Namers forced six turnovers in a 16–0 victory.

**Quarterback Earl Morrall started nine games for the Dolphins in 1972. He threw 11 touchdown passes.**

It was the first time in the Super Bowl

era that an NFL team had gone through a season undefeated. But the Dolphins weren't satisfied with regular-season success. After Kiick scored a late touchdown to beat the Cleveland Browns 20–14 in the divisional round of the playoffs, Miami hosted the Pittsburgh Steelers for the AFC title.

**Quarterback Bob Griese was Miami's first-round draft pick in 1967.**

Though Griese had returned in the regular-season finale, Morrall had played the entire Cleveland game and started against the Steelers as well. But the veteran couldn't get the offense going in the first half against Pittsburgh. Miami needed some trickery to get on the scoreboard. Late in the second quarter, Miami punter Larry Seiple, who also played tight end, took off from his own 40 on a fake. He gained 37 yards to set up a tying touchdown reception for Csonka.

The teams went into halftime still tied 7–7. Not satisfied, Shula switched to Griese. Though the quarterback didn't throw a touchdown pass, he led two scoring drives that Kiick finished off with short touchdown runs. Miami survived, 21-17.

## A SUPER FINALE

Super Bowl VII took place in Los Angeles. Despite their perfect 16-0 record, the Dolphins weren't heavy favorites against Washington. But Miami established both its offense and defense early. The Dolphins allowed only one first down on Washington's first two drives. And on the final play of the first quarter, Griese dropped a perfect pass between two defenders to tight end Howard Twilley, who dragged a defender into the end zone for a 28-yard touchdown.

**Miami defensive lineman Manny Fernandez stuffs Washington running back Larry Brown during Super Bowl VII after the 1972 season.**

The score remained 7–0 with two minutes left in the second quarter when Buoniconti, the Dolphins' vocal leader on defense, stepped in front of a pass and picked it off. He raced 32 yards to the Washington 24-yard line. Four plays later, Kiick pushed across a 1-yard score for a 14–0 lead.

The second half was a stalemate until Scott intercepted his second pass of the day with 5:33 left. This one came in the Miami end zone, and he sprinted 55 yards to set up the Dolphins' offense. Miami moved to the Washington 34-yard line and then sent Yepremian out for a 42-yard field goal attempt. Shula was on the

**Dolphins safety Jake Scott races out of the end zone after one of his interceptions in Super Bowl VII.**

**Miami kicker Garo Yepremian tries to throw a pass after his field goal attempt was blocked late in Super Bowl VII.**

sideline picturing the poetry of the moment. With a good kick, the Dolphins would cap their perfect 17–0 season with a 17–0 victory.

Yepremian, who was born on the European island of Cyprus, had played soccer before moving to the United States and teaching himself football. Normally one of the league's best kickers, he delivered a low line drive that Washington blocked. The panicked kicker then made matters worse by picking up the loose ball and trying to throw a pass. The ball bobbled out of his hands. Washington defensive back Mike Bass then grabbed the fumble and took it 49 yards for a score. Suddenly, Washington was within one touchdown, 14–7. An embarrassed Yepremian crept toward the sideline, hoping to avoid running into an angry Shula after committing one of the biggest blunders in Super Bowl history.

Washington got the ball back with 1:14 left. Once again the No-Name Defense stood tall. On fourth-and-14, Stanfill brought down Washington quarterback Billy Kilmer to end the game. Despite the scary finish, the Dolphins had completed their perfect season.

> "SEVENTEEN-AND-0 SAYS IT ALL. THE WORLD CHAMPIONSHIP. THE BEST TEAM EVER IN PROFESSIONAL FOOTBALL."
>
> —DON SHULA

At a rally back in Miami, Shula said to the crowd, "Seventeen-and-0 says it all. The world championship. The best team ever in professional football."

## TOASTING SUCCESS

Each year since their magical 1972 season, the surviving Dolphins have gathered for a celebration toast when the last remaining undefeated NFL team loses. The longest the team had to wait was in the 2007 season. That season, the New England Patriots took an 18–0 record into Super Bowl XLII before losing to the underdog New York Giants.

Bob Griese, *left*, and Don Shula, *right*, present President Barack Obama with a signed Dolphins jersey during a White House reception for the 1972 Miami team in 2013.

### ZONK

The Dolphins entered the 1973 season confident they could win it all again. In fact, many players considered the team better than the year before. The core of the roster returned, but the Dolphins now had one more year of championship experience and confidence.

The dream of a perfect season ended with a loss to the Raiders in Week 2. But Miami cruised to a 12–2 mark. Csonka, Morris, and Kiick once again paced one

The Dolphins get ready to carry coach Don Shula, *center*, off the field after finishing their perfect season.

of the league's top rushing offenses. Warfield pitched in by scoring 11 touchdowns despite catching only 29 passes all season. And the defense was no longer anonymous. Anderson won Defensive Player of the Year honors after intercepting eight passes and returning two for touchdowns. The Dolphins allowed the fewest points in the league once again.

All of Miami's stars showed up in the first round of the playoffs against the Cincinnati Bengals. By the end of the first quarter, Csonka, Morris, and Warfield had all scored touchdowns to build a

21–3 lead. Anderson added another interception as the Dolphins rolled to a 34–16 win.

Versatile running back Jim Kiick rushed for 257 yards and caught 27 passes for the Dolphins in 1973.

Miami didn't rely on one player, but for the rest of the playoffs, Csonka took over. The 6-foot-3-inch, 237-pound fullback was known as a punishing runner who barreled into defenders. Some of his teammates used to bet each game on which way Csonka's nose would be facing after smashing into tacklers.

Csonka usually gave more hits than he took. And in the AFC title game against the Raiders' rugged defense, Csonka plowed his way for an 11-yard touchdown in the first quarter and a 2-yard plunge in the second for a 14–0 lead. Though the Raiders tightened things up, Csonka finished his 29-carry, 117-yard day with a 1-yard touchdown in the fourth quarter to cap a 27–10 win.

**Running back Larry Csonka left the Dolphins as the team's all-time leading rusher with 6,737 career yards and 53 touchdowns.**

That victory put the Dolphins back in the Super Bowl, this time against the Minnesota Vikings. Known for their strong defensive line nicknamed "the Purple People Eaters," the Vikings had the league's second-best defense. But Miami got the ball first and fed the Vikings a steady diet of the fullback known as "Zonk."

Csonka carried the ball five times for 36 yards on the drive. On the last play, he took a handoff from Griese at the Vikings' 5 and burst through a hole. Two defenders hit Csonka at the 2, but he dragged them both into the end zone for a 6–0 lead.

The Dolphins continued to feed their hot hand for the rest of the game. When it was over, Csonka had rushed 33 times and scored twice. His Super Bowl record of 145 rushing yards stood for another nine years. The Dolphins crushed the hapless Vikings 24–7 and became the second team to win back-to-back Super Bowls.

## BIG NAMES

Despite the Dolphins' success, Joe Robbie was still one of the league's poorest owners. As his players came up for new contracts, he couldn't offer as much as other teams. The arrival of the World Football League (WFL) in 1974 only made things worse for Miami.

One way the WFL planned to compete with the NFL was by throwing big money at NFL free agents. The league came after Csonka, Kiick, and Warfield, luring them away with contracts that Robbie couldn't match. The stars' new deals weren't set to begin until 1975, however, so they played one more year with the Dolphins.

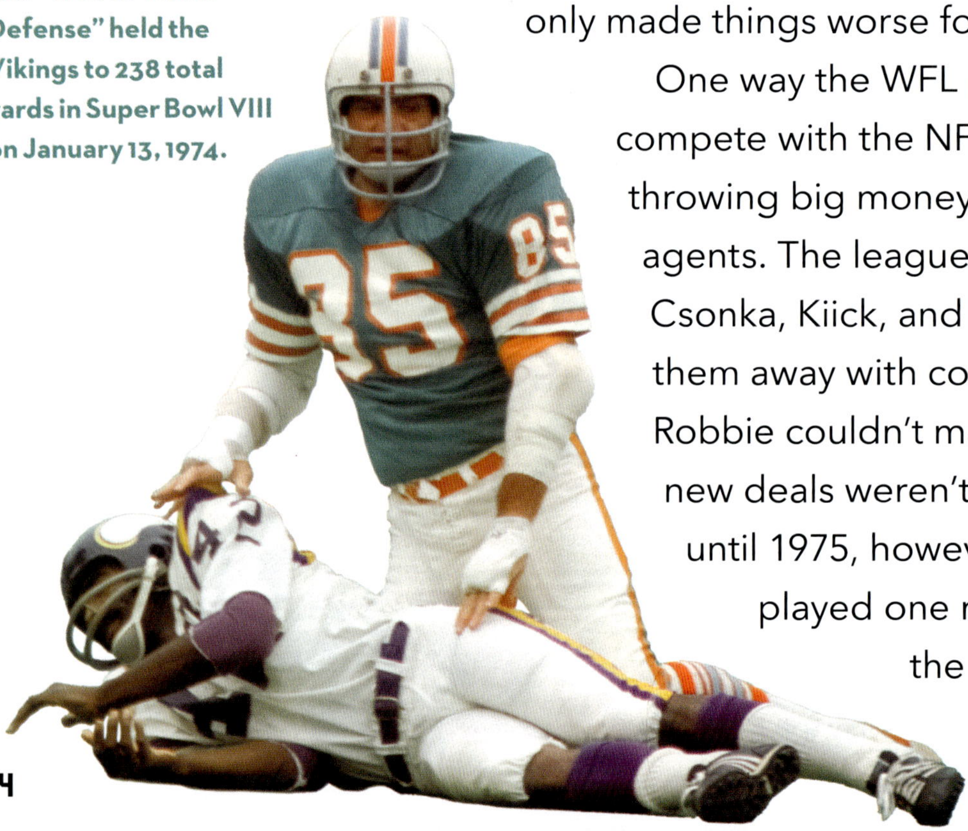

**Nick Buoniconti and "the No-Name Defense" held the Vikings to 238 total yards in Super Bowl VIII on January 13, 1974.**

Csonka barrels through two Minnesota Vikings for the first of his two touchdowns in Super Bowl VIII.

Seeking a third title, Miami battled through the distraction and won the AFC East with an 11–3 record. That set up a matchup between the Dolphins and Raiders in the divisional playoffs. Miami led 26–21 in the final minute when the Raiders faced fourth-and-goal from the Dolphins' 8. Den Herder pressured Oakland quarterback Ken Stabler, who tossed a desperation pass into a crowd of players in the end zone. With three Dolphins in the

Oakland Raiders running back Clarence Davis (28) makes his famous "Sea of Hands" catch to knock the Dolphins out of the playoffs after the 1974 season.

area, Raiders running back Clarence Davis somehow came down with the touchdown pass. The play that became known as "the Sea of Hands" ended Miami's championship run.

The stars left after that, and the Dolphins proved unable to get back to the top. They missed the playoffs in each of the next three seasons, even as they finished with winning records in two of them. Miami didn't win another playoff game for the rest of the 1970s.

Hall of Fame center Dwight Stephenson was drafted by the Dolphins in 1980. He went on to make the All-Pro team four times in his eight-year career.

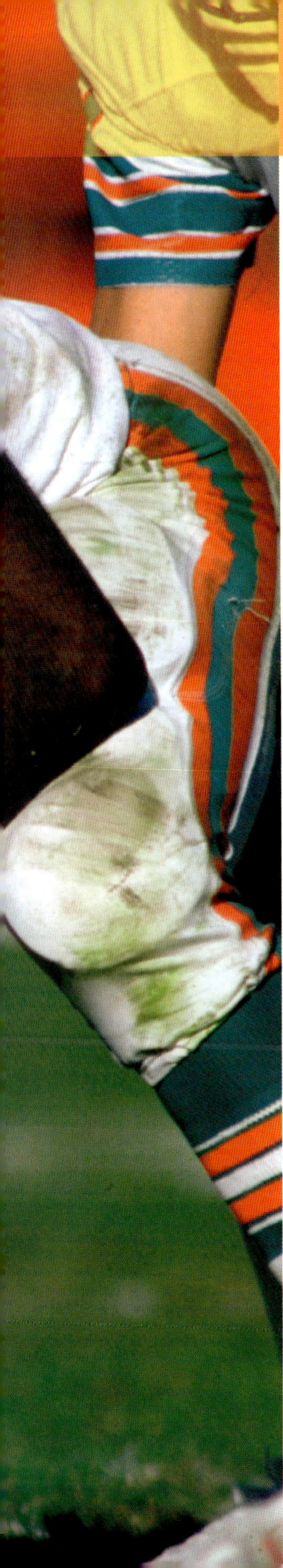

CHAPTER 4

# MIAMI MAGIC

**After the 1980 season, Bob Griese retired as the Dolphins'** quarterback. Though Griese had never put up huge numbers in the team's run-based offense, he was a well-respected team leader. Coach Don Shula knew that finding a new franchise quarterback wouldn't be easy.

Shula didn't replace Griese with one player. The Dolphins spent 1981 rotating between two quarterbacks. Twenty-three-year-old David Woodley was the starter. Woodley was a good runner but an inaccurate passer. So, the team designed several plays to take advantage of Woodley's athleticism. If Miami fell behind, veteran Don Strock came in for Woodley. With a stronger passing arm, Strock could air it out if the Dolphins needed to. The quarterback duo became known as "Woodstrock."

Woodstrock led the Dolphins to the AFC East title, and Miami hosted the San Diego Chargers in the divisional round of the playoffs. In the withering Miami heat, the teams played an all-time NFL classic. The Chargers built an early 24–0 lead, forcing Strock into the game. The veteran led a thrilling comeback. The highlight play came in the final minute of the first half. Strock threw a short pass to Duriel Harris at the San Diego 25-yard line. Harris then lateraled to running back Tony Nathan, who raced down the sideline for the score.

**Quarterback David Woodley throws a pass early in the Dolphins' playoff game against the San Diego Chargers on January 16, 1983.**

The famous play, called "Hook and Ladder," cut San Diego's lead to 24–17. It was one of four touchdown passes for Strock as Miami rallied to force overtime. However, San Diego blocked two potential game-winning kicks by the Dolphins' Uwe von Schamann in the extra period and eventually won "the Epic in Miami" 41–38.

The Dolphins still hadn't won a playoff game since Super Bowl VIII in January 1974.

## THE KILLER BEES

Despite allowing 41 points to the Chargers in their playoff game, the Dolphins still had an excellent defense. And that unit once again had a catchy nickname. Led by defensive linemen Bob Baumhower, Kim Bokamper, and Doug Betters, along with linebacker Bob Brudzinksi, and the brother tandem of Glenn and Lyle Blackwood at safety, the Dolphins' defense became known as "the Killer Bees."

The 1982 NFL season was cut to just nine games due to a players' strike over salaries. But the Killer Bees guided Miami to a 7–2 record

**"Killer Bees" defensive linemen Bob Baumhower, *left*, and Doug Betters, *right*, combined for 7 1/2 sacks during the 1982 season.**

by allowing just 14.6 points per game. In the playoffs, Miami routed the New England Patriots and took revenge on the Chargers with a 34–13 divisional-round win. That set up an AFC title game at the Orange Bowl against the New York Jets.

For three days before the game, heavy rain soaked the field. The mud-soaked field slowed down the Jets' speed-based offense, and the Killer Bees forced five turnovers. The biggest came in the fourth quarter by one of the "non-Bees." With Miami up 7–0, linebacker A. J. Duhe picked off his third pass of the day and ran 35 yards for a score. Miami won "the Mud Bowl" 14–0.

The Dolphins faced Washington in Super Bowl XVII. Ten years earlier, Miami had run over Washington on its way to a perfect season. This time, the Dolphins fell short. Led by lumbering running back John "Diesel" Riggins, Washington won 27–17.

## DAN THE MAN

The Dolphins completed a Super Bowl–low four passes in Super Bowl XVII. By 1983, it was clear that neither Woodley nor Strock could open up Miami's offense. Luckily, the Dolphins caught a break at the

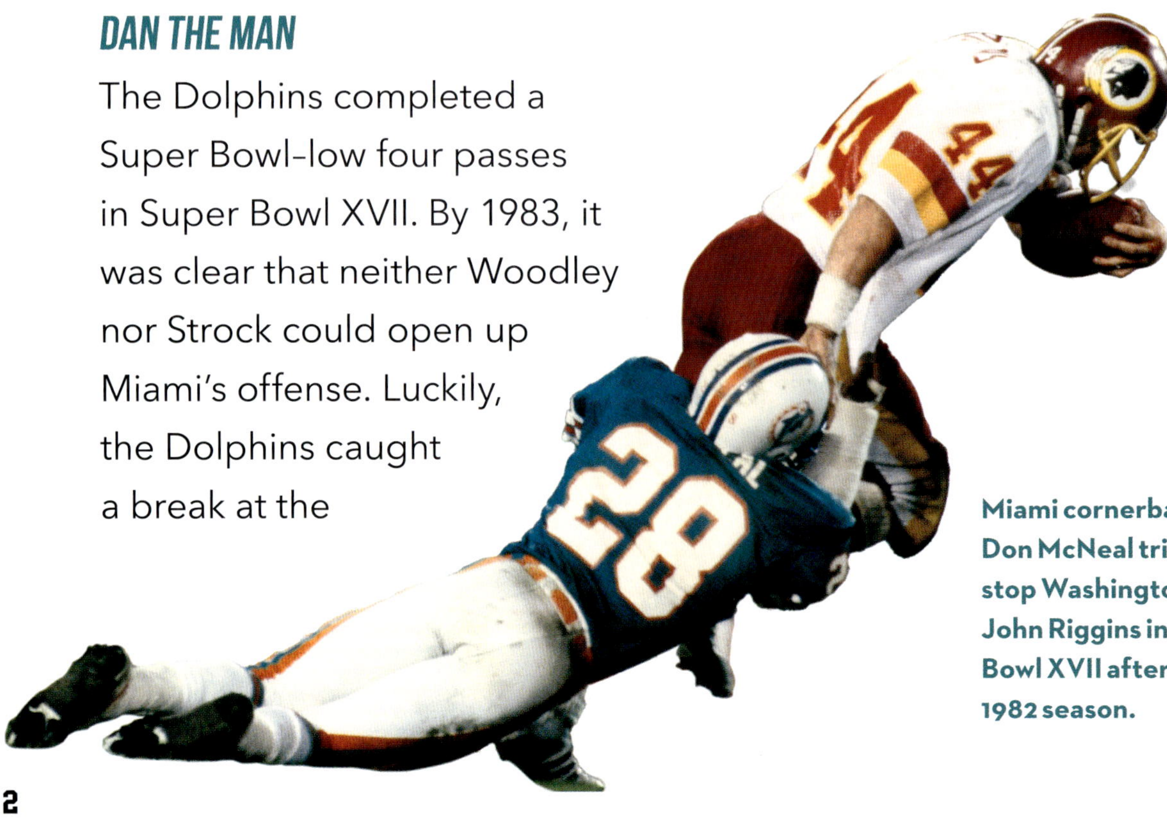

**Miami cornerback Don McNeal tries to stop Washington's John Riggins in Super Bowl XVII after the 1982 season.**

1983 draft. Many considered the group of incoming quarterbacks to be among the best of all time. Six ended up going in the first round.

Picking 27th, the Dolphins didn't have high hopes that they'd get one of them. Teams usually meet with players they're considering. Thinking he'd have no shot at Pittsburgh star Dan Marino, Miami coach Don Shula didn't bother. But when Marino unexpectedly remained available, the Dolphins snapped him up.

Dolphins quarterback Dan Marino throws a pass against the Seattle Seahawks during an AFC playoff game in December 1984.

Frustrated by falling so low, Marino showed up in Miami with a lot to prove. Overnight, he changed the way the Dolphins played. At 6 feet, 4 inches tall and 224 pounds, he was a big presence in the pocket. He combined that size with a rocket arm and one of the quickest releases scouts had ever seen. Marino didn't start for the first five games of the 1983 season, but when he took over, Miami was no longer a running team. In only nine starts, Marino threw for 2,210 yards and 20 touchdowns.

While his rookie numbers were impressive, Marino destroyed the NFL record books in 1984. Before that season, a quarterback had topped 4,000 passing yards in a season only seven times. Marino threw for 5,084. He also threw 48 touchdown passes, smashing the old record of 36.

Miami running back Tony Nathan looks for an opening during Super Bowl XIX after the 1984 season.

Marino's top target was Mark Clayton, who led the NFL with 18 touchdowns. On the other side, speedy Mark Duper racked up more than 1,300 yards on 71 receptions. When Marino wasn't throwing to "the Marks Brothers," he had plenty of completions left over for veteran receiver Nat Moore or Nathan out of the backfield. Later, Clayton said of Marino, "I can honestly say I played with The Man."

"I CAN HONESTLY SAY I PLAYED WITH THE MAN."

—MARK CLAYTON, ON DAN MARINO

The Dolphins finished 14-2 as opponents struggled to figure out the Miami passing machine. Marino didn't slow down in the playoffs either. In the divisional round, he tossed three touchdown passes in a 31-10 rout of the Seattle Seahawks. One week later, he threw four more scoring passes, with three of them coming on plays of longer than 30 yards. The Dolphins roughed up the Pittsburgh Steelers 45-28 to go back to the Super Bowl.

By the time Super Bowl XIX kicked off, many observers figured the game's record of 318 passing yards was sure to fall. Marino ended up tying the mark. However, San Francisco 49ers quarterback Joe Montana outshined Marino by throwing for 331 yards and three touchdowns. Marino's only scoring strike came on a 2-yard pass to tight end Dan Johnson in the first quarter. The play gave Miami a 10-7 lead, but the Dolphins' young quarterback spent the rest of the game fending

## PRESERVING PERFECTION

In Week 13 of the 1985 season, the Dolphins hosted the Chicago Bears. It was a huge game for Dolphins players past and present. The Bears entered the game 12-0 and were so dominant that many thought they could go undefeated. In front of a national television audience on *Monday Night Football*, Dan Marino threw three touchdown passes as Miami won 38-24 to preserve the 1972 Dolphins' legacy as the NFL's only perfect team.

Miami receiver Nat Moore celebrates a touchdown during the Dolphins' 1985 victory over the Chicago Bears.

off San Francisco's relentless pressure. The 49ers sacked Marino four times and intercepted him twice. His record-smashing season ended with a thud as the 49ers won 38–16.

Wide receiver Mark Clayton (83) played for the Dolphins from 1983 to 1992 and led the NFL in touchdown catches twice.

## PUZZLE PIECES

Most football fans figured Marino would get many more Super Bowl chances. And while he led the Dolphins back to the AFC title game after the 1985 season, they were stunned by the rival New England Patriots 31–14. Miami then surprisingly missed the postseason in five of the next six years.

Marino remained one of the league's best passers and most popular stars. He piled up endorsements as quickly as he did passing yards. He even played himself in a movie in the early 1990s. But the Dolphins' front office could never put the pieces together around their star quarterback. One of the biggest problems Miami had was the lack of a solid running game. In 1972, the Dolphins fielded two 1,000-yard rushers. But between 1979 and 1995, a Dolphins back topped 900 yards only twice. Without ground support, defenses keyed in on Marino and frustrated both the Dolphins' star and his head coach.

Shula and the Dolphins put together another big run in 1992. Marino, now 31 years old, topped 4,000 yards for the fifth time in his career. The Dolphins started 6-0 and, despite sputtering to a 5-5 finish, still won the AFC East.

The Dolphins hosted the San Diego Chargers in the divisional round of the playoffs. Though Marino threw for only 167 yards, he tossed three touchdown passes, including two to star tight end Keith Jackson. Miami's defense, led by fiery linebacker Bryan Cox, shut out the Chargers 31-0.

**Linebacker Bryan Cox had a career-high 14 sacks for the Dolphins in 1992.**

However, the next week, the Dolphins committed five turnovers against the division-rival Buffalo Bills. Buffalo routed Miami 29-10, stopping Marino and Shula one step short of the Super Bowl again. Time was running out for both legends.

Miami quarterback Dan Marino threw for 61,361 yards and 420 touchdowns in his 17-year career.

CHAPTER 5

# DOLPHIN TALES

**ON NOVEMBER 14, 1993, THE DOLPHINS ENTERED THE SECOND HALF** of a game against the Philadelphia Eagles trailing 14–13. In a defensive struggle, Miami scratched out two scoring drives. A pair of field goals by kicker Pete Stoyanovich gave the Dolphins a 19–14 edge that they never gave up. As the final whistle sounded, a handful of Miami players hoisted coach Don Shula up and carried him off the field. The win was the 325th of the legendary coach's career, breaking the record once held by George Halas of the Chicago Bears.

Dan Marino hadn't played in Shula's record-setting game. The star quarterback was out for the season with a torn Achilles tendon. He returned in 1994 and delivered Shula a wild-card playoff win by throwing two touchdowns in a 27–17 victory over the Kansas City Chiefs. It was

*"HE EMBODIED THE DEFINITION OF 'GREATNESS.' HE BROUGHT THAT WINNING ATTITUDE WITH HIM EVERY DAY AND MADE EVERYONE AROUND HIM BETTER."*

*—DAN MARINO, ON DON SHULA*

the last playoff victory of Shula's career. He retired after the 1995 season with 347 career wins.

"He embodied the definition of 'greatness,'" said Marino. "He brought that winning attitude with him every day and made everyone around him better."

## MARINO SIGNS OFF

Marino, too, was in the twilight of his career. Though his numbers weren't as big as they once were, he still guided the Dolphins and new coach Jimmy Johnson to the playoffs in the 1997, 1998, and 1999 seasons. But in the divisional round after the 1999 season, Marino's illustrious career came to an unfortunate end. The 38-year-old quarterback threw an interception on his first pass against the Jacksonville Jaguars. Later in the first quarter, he was sacked and fumbled. The Jaguars picked up the ball and scored. Marino threw another interception and lost another fumble in the second quarter. By the time he threw his first touchdown pass with nine seconds left in the half, Miami already trailed 41–0. Marino eventually came out of the 62–7 blowout loss early and retired after the season. The Hall of Fame quarterback left the NFL as its all-time leader in passing yards and touchdown passes.

With the face of the franchise gone, Miami fans had to latch on to new stars. There were plenty still around in south Florida. Middle linebacker Zach Thomas had joined the Dolphins as a fifth-round pick in 1996. Thomas was undersized and considered slow for the position. Not many expected him to become a star. But by the time

Defensive end Jason Taylor, *left*, and middle linebacker Zach Thomas, *right*, prepare for a snap during a game against the Indianapolis Colts in 2006.

he left the team in 2007, the intelligent Thomas had been named to five All-Pro teams on his way to the Hall of Fame.

Lining up in front of Thomas was Jason Taylor. The lightning-fast defensive end set the Dolphins' record with 18 1/2 sacks in 2002. Taylor excelled at bursting around helpless offensive linemen and stripping the ball from unsuspecting quarterbacks. In his career, Taylor forced 46 fumbles. He knocked loose an NFL-best nine in 2006 alone and was named the league's Defensive Player of the Year.

Running back Ricky Williams led the NFL in carries in 2002 and 2003.

On offense, Miami fans were awed by the running of Ricky Williams. After nearly two decades of poor results on the ground, Miami got a one-man show in Williams. The workhorse back joined the Dolphins in 2002 and immediately led the NFL with 1,853 rushing yards. He also ran for 16 touchdowns.

Though Williams was electric on the field, his heavy workload eventually burned him out. Just before training camp in 2004, he shockingly retired. He returned in 2005 before failing a drug test and getting suspended for the entire 2006 season. Williams came back once more and stayed with the Dolphins through 2010 but only once topped 1,000 yards.

## WILDCAT

While Miami had exciting players, the team wasn't winning. From 2001 to 2007, the Dolphins missed the playoffs every year. The 2007 team won only one game. The Dolphins needed big changes.

New coach Tony Sparano lost his first two games in 2008, and Week 3 looked like a tough matchup against the powerhouse New England Patriots. Led by coach Bill Belichick and quarterback Tom Brady, the Patriots had dominated the AFC East and won three Super Bowls since 2001. But Sparano's Dolphins put in a new wrinkle on offense. Quarterback Chad Pennington spent many plays on the sideline. In his place, Williams and fellow running back Ronnie Brown took snaps directly from the center. From there, they could either run, hand off to another running back, or even throw a pass.

Dolphins running back Ronnie Brown takes a snap out of the "Wildcat" formation during a game against the Seattle Seahawks in 2008.

**The Dolphins opened their home field in 1987 as Joe Robbie Stadium. It was renamed Hard Rock Stadium in 2016.**

The Patriots, known for their strong defense, were completely thrown off. Brown rushed for four touchdowns and threw another as the Dolphins rolled to a 38–13 victory.

Miami's new offense was called the "Wildcat." The team rode the strategy to an 11–5 record and a shocking AFC East title. It was the biggest one-season turnaround in NFL history. But in the playoffs' wild-card round, the Baltimore Ravens finally figured out Miami's scheme. Baltimore held the Dolphins to just 52 rushing yards as Miami lost 27–9.

## LOST AT SEA

Miami's surprising 2008 season wasn't a sign of things to come. In 2009, the Dolphins began a streak of four straight losing seasons.

Dolphins cornerback Vontae Davis celebrates an interception during a 2011 game.

General manager Jeff Ireland drew most of the blame. The team hadn't drafted well, and fans were frustrated. They began protesting at games, urging the team to let Ireland go. One group of fans even hired a plane to fly over the team's stadium displaying a "Fire Ireland" banner.

Miami fired Ireland after the 2014 season, but things didn't improve much. Despite a surprising 10–6 season in 2016 under first-year head coach Adam Gase, the Dolphins remained a mostly losing team. And winning didn't always guarantee a playoff spot.

Miami went 10-6 in 2020 but missed the postseason. The Dolphins missed out again in 2021 with a 9-8 record.

## HIGH-FLYING FINS

The Dolphins had only two head coaches between 1966 and 1995. But after Shula retired, Miami churned through 11 head coaches in 26 years. The team hired Mike McDaniel in 2022 to try to get the team back on top. At age 38, McDaniel became one of the youngest head coaches in the league. He was also considered one of the best offensive minds in football.

McDaniel put in a wide-open passing attack. And young quarterback Tua Tagovailoa gave the Dolphins their best passer since Dan Marino retired. Tagovailoa formed an instant connection with speedy receivers Tyreek Hill and Jaylen Waddle. The trio led Miami back to the playoffs in 2022 and again in 2023. But Miami lost its postseason opener in both

## THE MIRACLE IN MIAMI

In Week 14 of the 2018 season, the Dolphins trailed the visiting New England Patriots 33-27 with just seconds to play. Sitting at their own 31-yard line with time for only one more play, the Dolphins needed something special. Quarterback Ryan Tannehill threw a pass for receiver Kenny Stills. Stills then lateraled to DeVante Parker. Just as he was about to be tackled, Parker flipped the ball to Kenyan Drake. The running back wove past New England's defenders for a touchdown, completing "the Miracle in Miami" for a 34-33 win.

Kenyan Drake crosses the goal line to complete "the Miracle in Miami" in 2018 against the New England Patriots.

Miami wide receiver Jaylen Waddle makes a leaping touchdown catch in a 2023 game against the New York Giants.

# DOLPHINS TROPHY CASE

## SUPER BOWL CHAMPIONSHIPS: 2

Super Bowl VII – January 14, 1973
Super Bowl VIII – January 13, 1974

## CONFERENCE CHAMPIONSHIPS: 5

1971, 1972, 1973, 1982, 1984

## DIVISION TITLES: 14

**AFC East:** 1971, 1972, 1973, 1974, 1979, 1981, 1982, 1983, 1984, 1985, 1992, 1994, 2000, 2008

All stats are through the 2024 season.

**Quarterback Tua Tagovailoa, *right*, has thrived in Miami coach Mike McDaniel's pass-focused offense.**

seasons, meaning the team still hadn't won a playoff game since 2000. Then the team missed the playoffs altogether in 2024.

A big factor in two of those seasons was Tagovailoa's health. The young quarterback suffered three concussions between 2022 and 2024, including one that caused him to miss the team's playoff loss on January 15, 2023. After his fourth concussion, suffered early in the 2024 season, many former and current players told Tagovailoa that he should retire. Tagovailoa decided to return to the team and led the Dolphins to eight wins. With a healthy passer, Dolphins fans know their team has a shot to return to Miami's glory days. They just hope their star can stay on the field.

# TIMELINE

**1966**
The Dolphins are founded by lawyer Joe Robbie and actor/comedian Danny Thomas.

**1970**
Under new coach Don Shula, the Dolphins post their first winning season at 10-4.

**1972**
After a 10-3-1 season, the Dolphins advance to Super Bowl VI but lose 24-3 to the Dallas Cowboys on January 16.

**1973**
The Dolphins beat Washington 14-7 in Super Bowl VII on January 14, completing the NFL's first perfect season.

**1974**
The Dolphins repeat as Super Bowl champions by beating the Minnesota Vikings 24-7 in Super Bowl VIII on January 13.

**1983**
The Dolphins reach the Super Bowl but lose 27-17 to Washington on January 30.

Shula becomes the all-time winningest coach in NFL history.
**1993**

Marino retires as the NFL's all-time leader in passing yards and touchdowns.
**2000**

The Dolphins beat the New England Patriots on "the Miracle in Miami" play.
**2018**

**1985**
Led by record-setting quarterback Dan Marino, Miami reaches Super Bowl XIX on January 20 but loses 38-16 to the San Francisco 49ers.

**2008**
Using the "Wildcat" formation, the Dolphins win the AFC East one year after finishing 1-15.

**2023**
Despite missing a game, Tyreek Hill sets Miami's single-season record with 1,799 receiving yards.

# GLOSSARY

**contract**—an agreement to play for a certain team.

**coordinator**—an assistant coach who is in charge of the offense, defense, or special teams.

**draft**—a system that allows teams to acquire new players coming into the league.

**endorsement**—a deal in which an athlete promotes a company in exchange for the company's products or money.

**expansion team**—a new team that is added to an existing league.

**favorite**—the person or team that is expected to win.

**franchise**—an entire sports organization.

**free agent**—a player who is not signed to a team.

**general manager**—an executive who runs a team and is responsible for finding and signing players.

**lateral**—a pass that goes sideways or backward.

**overtime**—an extra period of play when the score is tied after regulation.

**players' strike**—a work stoppage due to a disagreement between players and their employers (teams) about things such as working conditions or wages.

**postseason**—another word for playoffs; the time after the end of the regular season when teams play to determine a champion.

**retire**—to end one's career.

**rival**—an opponent with whom a player or team has a fierce and ongoing competition.

**rookie**—a professional athlete in his or her first year of competition.

**sack**—a tackle of the quarterback behind the line of scrimmage before he can pass the ball.

**scout**—a person whose job is to look for talented young players.

**snap**—the start of each play, when the center hikes the ball between his legs to a player behind him, usually the quarterback.

**stalemate**—an even struggle.

**versatile**—able to perform many different roles or functions.

**veteran**—someone who has played for many years.

## ONLINE RESOURCES

Booklinks
NONFICTION NETWORK
FREE! ONLINE NONFICTION RESOURCES

To learn more about the Miami Dolphins, please visit **abdobooklinks.com** or scan this QR code. These links are routinely monitored and updated to provide the most current information available.

# INDEX